Mastering Clipchamp

Advanced Editing Tips & Tricks for Stunning Videos

Table of Contents:

1. Introduction to Advanced Editing in Clipchamp

- Overview of Clipchamp's capabilities
- Why go beyond basic editing?

2. Optimizing Your Workflow

- Customizing your workspace for efficiency
- Using keyboard shortcuts to speed up editing
- Best practices for project organization

3. Advanced Video Editing Techniques

- Multi-layer video editing
- Creating seamless transitions and overlays
- Using masks and blending modes creatively

4. Mastering Audio in Clipchamp

- Enhancing audio quality with advanced tools
- Syncing audio and video for professional results
- Adding sound effects and background music strategically

5. Color Grading & Visual Effects

- Using LUTs and custom color corrections
- Creating cinematic effects

- Adjusting exposure, contrast, and saturation for a professional look

6. Motion Graphics & Text Animation

- Customizing animated text templates
- Creating lower thirds and title sequences
- Using motion tracking for dynamic videos

7. Advanced Exporting & Optimization

- Choosing the best export settings for different platforms
- Reducing file size without losing quality
- Understanding frame rates and resolutions for different use cases

8. Clipchamp for Content Creators & Marketers

- Editing for YouTube, TikTok, and Instagram
- Best practices for engaging social media content
- Branding videos with logos and watermarks

9. AI-Powered Features & Automations

- Utilizing AI voiceovers
- Automatic captions and subtitles
- Smart background removal and enhancement

10. Troubleshooting & Performance Optimization

- Fixing common export and rendering issues
- Boosting Clipchamp performance on different devices
- Managing large files effectively

11. Bonus Tips & Hidden Features

- Easter eggs and lesser-known shortcuts
- Enhancing creativity with stock media and effects
- Community resources and further learning

Mastering Clipchamp

Advanced Editing Tips & Tricks for Stunning Videos

Chapter 1: Introduction to Advanced Editing in Clipchamp

Overview of Clipchamp's Capabilities

Clipchamp is a powerful and user-friendly video editing tool that caters to a wide range of users, from beginners to professionals. While its basic features make video editing accessible to all, its advanced functionalities allow users to create high-quality, engaging, and professional-grade content. Whether you're working on YouTube videos, marketing materials, tutorials, or personal projects, mastering Clipchamp's advanced tools can elevate your content to the next level.

Some of the key capabilities of Clipchamp include:

- **Multi-layer editing:** Enables precise control over multiple video and audio tracks.

- **Advanced text and motion effects:** Provides options for animated titles, subtitles, and callouts.
- **Green screen (Chroma keying):** Allows you to replace backgrounds and create stunning visual effects.
- **AI-powered tools:** Includes auto-captioning, text-to-speech, and voiceovers.
- **Stock media library:** Offers access to royalty-free videos, images, and soundtracks.
- **Custom branding:** Supports the addition of logos, watermarks, and brand-specific elements.
- **Speed and color adjustments:** Lets you fine-tune video pacing and color grading for cinematic effects.
- **Seamless integrations:** Works with platforms like Google Drive, Dropbox, and OneDrive for easy media access.

By exploring these features, you can unlock Clipchamp's full potential and create professional-quality videos without the need for expensive software or extensive editing experience.

Why Go Beyond Basic Editing?

Basic editing, such as trimming, cutting, and adding simple transitions, is sufficient for casual videos. However, if you want to make your videos more engaging, impactful, and professional, advanced editing techniques are essential. Here's why going beyond basic editing matters:

1. Enhanced Storytelling

Advanced editing techniques help in crafting compelling narratives. With multi-layer editing, special effects, and dynamic transitions, you can guide your audience through your content in a more engaging way.

2. Increased Engagement and Retention

Videos with smooth transitions, motion effects, and high-quality visuals are more likely to retain viewer attention. Studies show that well-edited videos have higher engagement rates, making them more effective for marketing, education, and entertainment.

3. Professional Appearance

A polished video with color correction, custom overlays, and precise audio synchronization stands out from amateur content. Whether you're a content creator, marketer, or educator, a professional-looking video enhances credibility and impact.

4. Better Social Media Performance

On platforms like YouTube, TikTok, and Instagram, high-quality videos tend to get more views, likes, and shares. Advanced editing allows you to optimize your content for each platform and create visually appealing videos that perform well.

5. Competitive Edge

With millions of videos uploaded daily, standing out requires more than just good content; it requires excellent execution. Advanced editing techniques set your videos apart from the competition, giving you a unique style and identity.

6. Greater Creative Control

Basic editing tools can be limiting, but advanced features allow for greater creativity. From cinematic effects to animated text and intricate audio layering, advanced editing empowers you to bring your vision to life exactly as you imagine it.

Conclusion

Mastering Clipchamp's advanced features is the key to creating high-quality videos that captivate and engage your audience. Whether you're looking to improve storytelling, boost viewer retention, or achieve a professional look, stepping beyond the basics will unlock new possibilities in video production. In the following chapters, we will explore these advanced tools and techniques in detail, helping you elevate your video editing skills to the next level.

Chapter 2: Optimizing Your Workflow

Efficiency is the key to mastering any video editing software, and Clipchamp is no exception. By customizing your workspace, leveraging keyboard shortcuts, and following best practices for project organization, you can streamline your workflow and complete projects faster with higher accuracy.

Customizing Your Workspace for Efficiency

Clipchamp offers a flexible workspace that can be tailored to suit your editing style. Personalizing the layout and settings will help you navigate the interface more efficiently and improve productivity. Here are some ways to customize your workspace for maximum efficiency:

1. Adjust the Timeline View

- Zoom in and out of the timeline using the zoom slider to get a detailed or broad view of your clips.
- Expand or minimize the timeline sections to focus on specific areas of your project.

2. Organize the Media Library

- Create folders to categorize different assets such as raw footage, background music, overlays, and transitions.

- Use tags or rename files to make searching for elements quicker.

3. Personalize the Editing Panel

- Rearrange or resize panels based on your preference to prioritize frequently used tools.
- Pin commonly used effects, transitions, and templates for quick access.

4. Enable Auto-Save and Backup Options

- Ensure auto-save is enabled to prevent data loss.
- Save a copy of your project to the cloud or an external drive for backup.

Using Keyboard Shortcuts to Speed Up Editing

Keyboard shortcuts are a powerful way to accelerate your editing workflow. Instead of relying solely on mouse clicks, using shortcut keys can significantly reduce the time spent on repetitive tasks. Here are some essential Clipchamp shortcuts to enhance your efficiency:

Basic Editing Shortcuts:

- **Ctrl + Z** – Undo
- **Ctrl + Y** – Redo
- **Ctrl + C** – Copy
- **Ctrl + V** – Paste
- **Delete** – Remove selected clip

Timeline Navigation:

- **Spacebar** – Play/Pause the timeline
- **Arrow Left/Right** – Move the playhead frame by frame
- **Home** – Jump to the beginning of the timeline
- **End** – Jump to the end of the timeline

Clip Manipulation:

- **S** – Split a clip at the playhead
- **R** – Rotate selected clip
- **T** – Add text to the timeline
- **G** – Group selected clips together

Speed & Productivity:

- **Ctrl + S** – Save the project
- **Ctrl + Shift + E** – Export video
- **Ctrl + Shift + N** – Create a new project

By incorporating these shortcuts into your editing process, you can make quick adjustments and maintain a smooth workflow.

Best Practices for Project Organization

A well-organized project ensures efficiency and reduces the risk of errors. Structuring your workflow methodically will help you stay on track and avoid confusion, especially when working on larger projects. Follow these best practices for project organization:

1. Name Your Project Clearly

Give your project a descriptive name that reflects its content, such as **"Travel Vlog_Europe 2025"**, to make it easily identifiable.

2. Use a Consistent File Naming System

When importing assets, use clear and consistent file names, such as **"Interview_Scene1.mp4"** or **"BackgroundMusic_Piano.mp3"**, instead of generic names like **"Clip001"**.

3. Create a Logical Folder Structure

Organize your files into separate folders:

- **Footage:** Store raw videos and b-roll footage.
- **Audio:** Keep voiceovers, music, and sound effects.
- **Graphics:** Store overlays, animations, and images.
- **Exports:** Save finalized videos in different versions if necessary.

4. Color-Code Your Clips

Use color labels to differentiate between various types of clips, such as interviews, transitions, or special effects. This makes it easier to identify specific elements within the timeline.

5. Maintain Version Control

- Save multiple versions of your project to track progress and prevent accidental loss of changes.
- Label versions numerically or by date, such as **"Project_v1.0"** or **"Project_2025_02_21"**.

6. Regularly Review and Clean Up Your Timeline

- Delete unnecessary clips and unused assets to declutter your workspace.
- Review the sequence to ensure smooth transitions and proper alignment of clips.

By following these workflow optimization techniques, you can enhance your editing speed, improve organization, and ensure a seamless video creation experience in Clipchamp. Mastering these skills will allow you to produce high-quality content with less effort and greater efficiency.

Chapter 3: Advanced Video Editing Techniques

Multi-Layer Video Editing

Multi-layer video editing is an essential skill for creating professional-grade videos. It allows editors to stack multiple elements such as footage, text, images, effects, and animations within a single timeline. By mastering this technique, you can enhance storytelling, improve visual appeal, and create complex compositions.

Understanding Layers

In most video editing software, the timeline consists of multiple tracks that function similarly to layers in image editing programs. The topmost layers in the stack take visual priority, while lower layers are visible when the upper layers contain transparency or blending effects.

Organizing Layers Efficiently

1. **Primary Footage Layer:** Always keep your main video clips on one of the lower layers to maintain clarity.
2. **Text and Graphics:** Use separate layers for titles, subtitles, and overlays to control their position and movement independently.
3. **Effects and Enhancements:** Apply effects to dedicated layers to maintain flexibility and easy adjustments.
4. **Adjustment Layers:** Some editing software allows adjustment layers, which let you apply

color grading and effects globally across multiple clips without modifying the original footage.

Practical Example

Suppose you're creating a cinematic sequence with a subject in the foreground and a background effect, such as a lens flare.

1. Place the main footage on **Track 1**.
2. Add a transparent overlay with a lens flare effect on **Track 2**.
3. If needed, include a color correction adjustment layer on **Track 3** to unify the color grading.
4. Finally, add a title animation on **Track 4** to complete the composition.

With this method, you ensure that all elements remain editable, and modifications can be made without disrupting the entire timeline.

Creating Seamless Transitions and Overlays

Transitions and overlays enhance the smoothness and professional appeal of videos. Properly executed transitions ensure that scene changes feel natural rather than jarring.

Types of Transitions

1. **Cut:** The simplest and most used transition, where one clip instantly replaces another.
2. **Dissolve:** A gradual fade from one clip to another, often used in storytelling to show time progression.
3. **Wipe:** One clip pushes another off the screen in a directional movement.
4. **Zoom and Scale Transitions:** A zoom-in or zoom-out effect that seamlessly transitions between clips, often used in travel and action videos.
5. **Glitch and Distortion Transitions:** Modern transitions that create a digital malfunction effect, perfect for high-tech or futuristic themes.

Crafting Custom Transitions

To create a smooth custom transition:

1. **Overlay a Pre-Designed Transition Effect:** Use third-party plugins or built-in presets.
2. **Use Keyframes for Animation:** Manually animate opacity, position, or scale changes between two clips.
3. **Blend Frames Using Optical Flow:** Some software offers AI-driven optical flow to create motion-blurred transitions.
4. **Layered Motion Graphics:** Introduce a moving element, such as light leaks or speed ramps, to enhance the transition effect.

Overlay Techniques

Overlays add depth and creativity to videos. Common overlay techniques include:

- **Light Leaks:** Soft, glowing transitions that add warmth to footage.
- **Grain and Film Effects:** Adds a vintage or cinematic feel.
- **Double Exposure:** Merging two different shots with blending modes for a surreal effect.
- **HUD & Motion Graphics:** Useful in tech-related videos to create an augmented reality look.

Example: Adding a subtle **bokeh overlay** during a romantic scene enhances the dreamlike quality of the footage.

Using Masks and Blending Modes Creatively

Masks and blending modes are powerful tools that allow you to isolate parts of an image or create complex compositions with multiple clips.

Masking Techniques

Masking lets you selectively show or hide portions of a layer. Common masking applications include:

1. **Object Isolation:** Cut out objects from the background for compositing.

2. **Text Reveal Effects:** Animate text to appear behind or through objects.
3. **Split-Screen Effects:** Display multiple videos side by side or within shapes.
4. **Motion Tracking Masks:** Apply a mask that follows a subject's movement.

How to Create a Mask:

1. Select your clip and access the masking tool.
2. Use the pen tool or shape tool to define the mask area.
3. Adjust feathering and opacity for a seamless look.
4. If needed, apply keyframes to animate the mask over time.

Blending Modes

Blending modes determine how a layer interacts with those beneath it. Some commonly used blending modes include:

- **Multiply:** Darkens the image by blending it with the layer below.
- **Screen:** Lightens the image, often used for glow effects.
- **Overlay:** Increases contrast while blending colors naturally.
- **Difference:** Creates a negative color effect, useful for creative edits.

Example: Creating a Double Exposure Effect

1. Place your **main subject** video on Track 1.
2. Add a **nature or cityscape video** on Track 2.

3. Apply the **Screen or Overlay** blending mode.
4. Mask out areas where you want the subject to stand out.
5. Adjust opacity and feathering for a smooth transition.

This technique is commonly used in music videos and artistic projects to create a dreamy, surreal look.

Conclusion

Mastering multi-layer editing, seamless transitions, and creative use of masks and blending modes can significantly elevate the quality of your video projects. By experimenting with these advanced techniques, you can produce engaging and visually stunning content that stands out from the crowd.

Chapter 4: Mastering Audio in Clipchamp

Audio is an essential component of any professional-quality video. Whether you're creating content for social media, marketing videos, or personal projects, clear and well-balanced sound can elevate your production. In this chapter, we will explore advanced techniques to enhance audio quality, sync audio and video seamlessly, and strategically incorporate sound effects and background music in Clipchamp.

Enhancing Audio Quality with Advanced Tools

Poor audio quality can make even the most visually stunning video appear unprofessional. Fortunately, Clipchamp provides several tools to enhance your audio:

1. Noise Reduction

Unwanted background noise can be distracting. Clipchamp includes a noise reduction feature to help clean up your audio. To use this feature:

- Select the audio clip in your timeline.
- Click on the **Audio tab** in the editing menu.
- Enable **Noise Reduction** and adjust the intensity to find the right balance.

2. Audio Equalizer

The equalizer (EQ) allows you to adjust different frequency ranges to improve clarity and tone.

- Select the audio clip.
- Click **Effects** and choose **Equalizer**.
- Use presets like "Bass Boost" or "Treble Boost," or manually adjust frequencies for a customized sound.

3. Volume Normalization

If your audio levels are inconsistent, normalization helps maintain a uniform volume across all clips.

- Right-click the audio clip and choose **Adjust Audio**.
- Select **Normalize Volume** to ensure a balanced sound.

4. Reverb and Echo Effects

For creative audio styling, you can add reverb and echo effects to enhance voiceovers, music, or ambient sounds.

- Select your clip, go to **Audio Effects**, and experiment with different settings.

Syncing Audio and Video for Professional Results

Proper audio-video synchronization ensures that spoken words align with lip movements and background music complements the visuals. Here are some tips to achieve perfect synchronization in Clipchamp:

1. Manually Aligning Audio

- Drag and drop your audio and video clips onto the timeline.
- Zoom into the timeline for precision.
- Drag the audio track left or right to align it with the visuals.

2. Using the Waveform as a Guide

Clipchamp displays waveforms for audio tracks, which help you match audio peaks to corresponding video actions.

- Enable the waveform view in the **Audio tab**.
- Match key peaks (e.g., claps, speech patterns) to visual cues.

3. Adjusting Audio Speed

If your audio is slightly off, you can speed up or slow down the clip to align it with the video.

- Select the audio clip, click **Speed**, and adjust accordingly.

4. Lip Syncing Tips

- Record high-quality audio separately and import it into Clipchamp.
- Use markers on the timeline to match key words or sounds.
- Play the video back multiple times to fine-tune alignment.

Adding Sound Effects and Background Music Strategically

Background music and sound effects can enhance storytelling and create emotional impact. Here's how to use them effectively:

1. Choosing the Right Background Music

The right music sets the tone for your video. Clipchamp provides a library of royalty-free tracks or allows you to upload your own.

- Navigate to **Stock Library** > **Music & SFX**.
- Preview and select a track that complements your video's mood.
- Drag it onto the timeline and adjust the length as needed.

2. Volume Mixing for Balance

Music should enhance, not overpower, the dialogue or narration.

- Use the **Audio Mixing** tool to lower music volume when speech occurs.
- Fade in and fade out music for smoother transitions.

3. Adding Sound Effects

Sound effects add realism and engagement.

- Browse the **Sound Effects** section in the **Stock Library**.
- Choose effects like footsteps, explosions, or ambient sounds.
- Layer them on the timeline and adjust their position for realism.

4. Using Audio Transitions

Smooth audio transitions prevent abrupt changes between clips.

- Apply **Fade In** and **Fade Out** effects by adjusting the audio clip edges.
- Crossfade two overlapping audio clips for seamless blending.

Conclusion

Mastering audio in Clipchamp transforms your videos from ordinary to professional. By enhancing audio quality, ensuring precise synchronization, and strategically using music and sound effects, you create an engaging and immersive experience for your audience.

Chapter 5: Color Grading & Visual Effects

Color grading and visual effects are essential components in post-production that can transform raw footage into a visually captivating story. This chapter delves into the tools and techniques used to create a professional and cinematic look, covering everything from LUTs and custom color corrections to fine-tuning exposure, contrast, and saturation.

---

1. Introduction

In the digital filmmaking landscape, the visual tone of your project plays a crucial role in conveying mood and emotion. Color grading not only enhances the aesthetic quality but also reinforces narrative themes. Whether you're aiming for a stark, high-contrast drama or a warm, nostalgic tale, the right color palette can elevate your work to the next level.

---

2. Using LUTs (Look-Up Tables)

What Are LUTs?

LUTs are predefined color profiles that map one set of colors to another, allowing you to apply a consistent look across your project. They serve as a starting point

23

in the color grading process, ensuring that each scene maintains visual consistency.

Benefits of Using LUTs

- **Efficiency:** Quickly achieve a baseline look without extensive manual adjustments.
- **Consistency:** Maintain a uniform color scheme across multiple scenes.
- **Creative Exploration:** Experiment with different styles by swapping LUTs to see how each one affects your footage.

Practical Application

1. **Selection:** Choose a LUT that aligns with the emotional tone of your narrative. Many professional LUT libraries cater to various genres.
2. **Application:** Import your LUT into your editing software. Apply it to an adjustment layer for non-destructive editing.
3. **Fine-Tuning:** After applying a LUT, adjust additional parameters to refine the look. A LUT is rarely a one-size-fits-all solution, so adjustments in exposure, contrast, and saturation might still be necessary.

3. Custom Color Corrections

The Importance of Customization

While LUTs provide a quick start, custom color corrections allow for granular control over your footage. Every shot is unique, and custom corrections help tailor the color grading process to suit specific lighting conditions, skin tones, and artistic visions.

Key Techniques

- **Primary Color Correction:** Adjust the overall balance of shadows, midtones, and highlights. This step ensures that the base image is properly balanced.
- **Secondary Color Correction:** Focus on individual elements within a scene, such as enhancing the blue of the sky or the warmth of a sunset. This often involves isolating specific color ranges using masks or keying tools.
- **Shot Matching:** When working with footage from different cameras or varying lighting conditions, custom corrections are necessary to create a seamless flow between shots.

Tools and Software

Popular color grading software like DaVinci Resolve, Adobe Premiere Pro, and Final Cut Pro offer robust color correction tools. These platforms allow you to manipulate curves, color wheels, and selective adjustments for precision work.

4. Creating Cinematic Effects

The Role of Cinematic Effects

Cinematic effects go beyond basic corrections, adding stylistic elements that contribute to the overall narrative feel. These effects can help simulate the visual cues typically associated with film, such as film grain, vignettes, and dynamic lighting adjustments.

Techniques to Enhance Cinematic Quality

- **Film Grain:** Introduce subtle grain to mimic the texture of film stock, which can add depth and an organic feel to digital footage.
- **Vignettes:** Use vignetting to focus the viewer's attention towards the center of the frame. This technique can enhance the mood by darkening the edges of the frame.
- **Light Leaks and Flares:** Simulate lens flares or light leaks to give a scene a more ethereal or dreamlike quality.
- **Depth of Field Adjustments:** Emulate a shallow depth of field by selectively blurring parts of the image, which can create a sense of intimacy and focus on key subjects.

Balancing Effects with Reality

While cinematic effects can greatly enhance the storytelling, they must be applied judiciously. Overuse can distract from the narrative and make the footage look overly processed. The goal is to complement the story, not overshadow it.

5. Adjusting Exposure, Contrast, and Saturation

Exposure

Exposure adjustments are critical to ensure that your image is neither too dark nor too bright. Correct exposure lays the foundation for further color grading.

- **Highlight Recovery:** Adjust highlights to recover details in bright areas.
- **Shadow Enhancement:** Lift shadow details to reveal nuances in darker areas without losing the overall mood.

Contrast

Contrast affects the difference between the light and dark areas of your image, contributing to the overall dynamism and depth.

- **Dynamic Range:** Enhance contrast to boost the dynamic range and give the image more punch.
- **Balanced Look:** Ensure that contrast adjustments don't crush the blacks or blow out the whites, maintaining detail in both extremes.

Saturation

Saturation controls the intensity of colors, influencing the mood and emotional impact of your footage.

- **Subtle Enhancement:** Increase saturation to make colors pop, especially in vibrant scenes.
- **Desaturation for Mood:** Reduce saturation for a more subdued, dramatic look when the narrative calls for it.
- **Skin Tones:** Special attention must be given to skin tones, ensuring they remain natural and true to life, which often involves selective saturation adjustments.

6. Integrating the Techniques for a Professional Look

Workflow and Best Practices

1. **Start with a Solid Base:** Begin by ensuring your footage is correctly exposed and balanced.
2. **Apply a LUT:** Use a LUT to establish a foundational look that fits your project's style.
3. **Fine-Tune with Custom Corrections:** Adjust specific areas that need refinement, using primary and secondary color correction tools.
4. **Enhance with Cinematic Effects:** Introduce creative elements such as film grain and vignettes sparingly to elevate the cinematic quality.
5. **Iterate and Review:** Continuously review your footage on different monitors and under varied lighting conditions. Iteration is key to achieving the desired professional look.

Final Thoughts

Color grading and visual effects are not just technical processes; they are artistic endeavors that allow filmmakers to express their vision. By mastering the use of LUTs, custom corrections, and cinematic enhancements, you can transform your footage into a compelling visual narrative that resonates with your audience.

Chapter 6: Motion Graphics & Text Animation

Motion graphics and text animation are essential techniques for creating engaging videos. Whether you're working on a promotional video, a tutorial, or a film, well-designed motion graphics can add a professional touch. In this chapter, we'll explore how to customize animated text templates, create lower thirds and title sequences, and use motion tracking for dynamic videos.

6.1 Customizing Animated Text Templates

Most modern video editing software, including **DaVinci Resolve, Adobe Premiere Pro, and Final Cut Pro**, provide pre-made animated text templates. These templates serve as a foundation for creating professional-looking text animations without starting from scratch.

Steps to Customize Animated Text Templates:

1. **Import the Template** – In your video editing software, navigate to the text or motion graphics library and select a template.
2. **Modify the Text** – Double-click on the text field to edit it with your desired content.

3. **Adjust the Font & Size** – Use the text properties panel to change the font, size, and spacing.
4. **Customize Colors** – Modify text and background colors to align with your branding.
5. **Animate Additional Elements** – Add effects such as fade-ins, slide-ins, or rotations for extra visual appeal.
6. **Fine-tune Motion Speed** – Adjust keyframe timing to make the animation smoother.
7. **Export and Preview** – Always preview the animation to ensure smooth motion before rendering.

Tip: If you're using Adobe After Effects, consider using **Motion Blur** to create more natural text transitions.

6.2 Creating Lower Thirds and Title Sequences

What Are Lower Thirds?

Lower thirds are graphics that appear in the lower section of a video frame, typically displaying the speaker's name, title, or relevant information. These are commonly used in news broadcasts, interviews, and documentaries.

How to Create Lower Thirds:

1. **Create a Text Layer** – Insert a new text layer in your video editor.

2. **Design a Background Box** – Add a solid rectangle shape behind the text for contrast.
3. **Apply Motion Effects** – Use keyframes to animate the entry and exit of the lower third.
4. **Use Opacity and Fades** – A subtle fade-in effect makes the graphic appear smoothly.
5. **Ensure Readability** – Keep the text clear and concise with high contrast against the video background.
6. **Save as a Preset** – If you create lower thirds frequently, save your design as a reusable preset.

Title Sequences

Title sequences set the tone for a video, often appearing at the beginning of movies, vlogs, and presentations. A strong title sequence should:

- Have a visually appealing font and animation style.
- Include motion elements such as zoom-ins, fades, or 3D rotations.
- Utilize background effects like light leaks or gradients for a cinematic look.

Tip: Use **After Effects or DaVinci Resolve Fusion** to create more advanced title sequences with particle effects and complex animations.

6.3 Using Motion Tracking for Dynamic Videos

Motion tracking is a powerful technique that allows text or graphics to follow the movement of an object in a video. This feature is useful for labeling objects, creating dynamic callouts, or adding interactive elements.

Steps to Use Motion Tracking:

1. **Select Your Footage** – Import a video clip with a clear moving object.
2. **Choose a Tracking Tool** – In After Effects, Premiere Pro, or DaVinci Resolve, select the motion tracking feature.
3. **Set a Tracking Point** – Click on the object you want to track and let the software analyze the movement.
4. **Attach Text or Graphics** – Link your text or image layer to the tracking data.
5. **Refine the Motion Path** – Adjust keyframes if necessary to smooth out inconsistencies.
6. **Apply Final Effects** – Add shadows, outlines, or glow to integrate the text naturally into the scene.

Example Use Case: Imagine a travel video where a moving car is labeled with animated text that stays attached to the vehicle as it moves across the frame.

Conclusion

Motion graphics and text animation add vibrancy and professionalism to video content. By customizing animated templates, designing lower thirds and title sequences, and using motion tracking, you can create engaging and visually stunning videos. Mastering these techniques will set your videos apart and elevate your storytelling capabilities.

Chapter 7: Advanced Exporting & Optimization

Exporting is the final and one of the most crucial stages in the video production process. Choosing the right export settings ensures that your content looks its best across different platforms while maintaining an optimal balance between quality and file size. In this chapter, we will explore the best export settings for various platforms, techniques for reducing file size without losing quality, and how to understand frame rates and resolutions for different use cases.

1. Introduction

After editing and color grading, the next step is exporting your video in a format that best suits your target audience. The wrong export settings can result in a video that looks pixelated, stutters during playback, or takes too long to upload. By optimizing your export settings, you ensure that your video retains its quality while remaining efficient in file size and compatibility.

2. Choosing the Best Export Settings for Different Platforms

Each platform has different recommended video specifications, so choosing the right settings is essential for quality and performance. Below are the optimal export settings for various platforms:

YouTube & Vimeo

- **Format:** MP4 (H.264 codec)
- **Resolution:** 1080p (1920x1080) or 4K (3840x2160)
- **Frame Rate:** 24, 30, or 60 FPS (Match original footage)
- **Bitrate:**
  - **1080p:** 8-12 Mbps
  - **4K:** 35-45 Mbps
- **Audio:** AAC, 320 kbps, 48kHz

Instagram (Reels, Stories, IGTV, Feed)

- **Format:** MP4 (H.264 codec)
- **Resolution:**
  - **Feed & IGTV:** 1080x1350 (4:5) or 1080x1920 (9:16)
  - **Stories & Reels:** 1080x1920 (9:16)
- **Frame Rate:** 30 or 60 FPS
- **Bitrate:** 5-10 Mbps
- **Audio:** AAC, 128 kbps or higher, 44.1kHz

TikTok

- **Format:** MP4 (H.264 codec)
- **Resolution:** 1080x1920 (9:16)
- **Frame Rate:** 30 or 60 FPS
- **Bitrate:** 5-10 Mbps
- **Audio:** AAC, 128 kbps or higher, 44.1kHz

Facebook

- **Format:** MP4 (H.264 codec)
- **Resolution:** 1080p (1920x1080)
- **Frame Rate:** 30 FPS
- **Bitrate:** 6-8 Mbps
- **Audio:** AAC, 128 kbps or higher, 44.1kHz

Twitter/X

- **Format:** MP4 (H.264 codec)
- **Resolution:** 1280x720 (16:9) or 1080x1080 (Square)
- **Frame Rate:** 30 FPS
- **Bitrate:** 5 Mbps
- **Audio:** AAC, 128 kbps, 44.1kHz

LinkedIn

- **Format:** MP4 (H.264 codec)
- **Resolution:** 1920x1080 (16:9)
- **Frame Rate:** 30 FPS
- **Bitrate:** 5-10 Mbps
- **Audio:** AAC, 128 kbps or higher

Exporting for Professional Use (Broadcast & Film)

- **Format:** ProRes (Apple ProRes 422 HQ or ProRes 4444)
- **Resolution:** 4K or higher
- **Frame Rate:** 24 FPS (cinematic) or 30 FPS (TV)
- **Bitrate:** High-quality (50+ Mbps)
- **Audio:** Uncompressed WAV or AIFF, 48kHz or higher

3. Reducing File Size Without Losing Quality

Large file sizes can cause issues with storage, sharing, and uploading times. However, reducing file size without sacrificing quality requires a balance between compression and resolution.

Techniques for File Size Optimization

1. Use Efficient Codecs

The H.265 (HEVC) codec provides better compression than H.264 while maintaining the same quality, reducing file sizes by up to 50%. However, not all platforms support H.265, so verify before using it.

2. Adjust Bitrate Settings

Bitrate determines how much data is used per second of video. Lowering the bitrate can drastically reduce file size, but too much reduction will cause quality loss.

- **Variable Bitrate (VBR):** Allows bitrate to adjust dynamically, optimizing file size.
- **Constant Bitrate (CBR):** Maintains a steady bitrate but may result in larger files.
- **Recommended Bitrate Ranges:**
    - 1080p: **8-12 Mbps** (VBR)
    - 4K: **35-45 Mbps** (VBR)

3. Lower the Resolution (If Needed)

If high resolution isn't required, exporting at 1080p instead of 4K can significantly reduce file size while maintaining good quality.

4. Reduce Frame Rate (If Suitable)

For non-action-heavy videos, reducing the frame rate from 60 FPS to 30 FPS can cut file size without noticeable quality loss.

5. Optimize Audio Settings

Use compressed audio formats like AAC instead of uncompressed WAV files to reduce file size while keeping audio quality high.

---

4. Understanding Frame Rates and Resolutions for Different Use Cases

Frame rates and resolutions play a significant role in how your video appears on different screens and platforms. Choosing the wrong settings can lead to choppy playback or unnecessary file bloat.

Frame Rates Explained

- **24 FPS (Frames Per Second):** Standard for films, provides a cinematic feel.

- **30 FPS:** Common for social media and online videos.
- **60 FPS:** Used for high-motion content like gaming, sports, and action videos.
- **120+ FPS:** Used for slow-motion shots to maintain smooth playback.

Choosing the Right Resolution

- **480p (854x480):** Low-quality, used for small mobile screens or quick previews.
- **720p (1280x720):** Standard definition for online videos with low bandwidth.
- **1080p (1920x1080):** Full HD, the most commonly used resolution for social media and professional work.
- **4K (3840x2160):** High-quality videos for YouTube, professional filmmaking, and future-proofing content.
- **8K (7680x4320):** Ultra-high resolution used for top-tier filmmaking and special applications.

5. Final Exporting Checklist

Before finalizing your export, go through this checklist to ensure the best possible output:

- **Confirm the target platform's recommended settings.**
- **Choose the right format (MP4 for online, ProRes for professional work).**
- **Optimize file size by adjusting bitrate and resolution.**

- **Ensure correct frame rate (24 FPS for cinematic, 30 FPS for online, 60 FPS for action).**
- **Check audio settings (AAC 128-320 kbps for best balance of quality and size).**
- **Test playback on different devices to ensure compatibility.**

6. Conclusion

Optimizing export settings is crucial for ensuring your video looks professional while remaining efficient in size and compatibility. By selecting the right format, codec, bitrate, and resolution, you can maximize quality while keeping file sizes manageable. Whether you're uploading to YouTube, posting on Instagram, or preparing for a professional film project, these export techniques will help you deliver polished, high-quality content.

Chapter 8: Clipchamp for Content Creators & Marketers

Introduction

In the fast-paced world of digital marketing and content creation, video is a crucial tool for engagement and brand visibility. Platforms like YouTube, TikTok, and Instagram thrive on high-quality, engaging content that captures attention within seconds. Clipchamp provides an intuitive and powerful video editing solution tailored for creators and marketers looking to produce professional content without the need for expensive software or steep learning curves. This chapter will explore how to use Clipchamp effectively for social media content creation, including best practices for engagement and branding videos with logos and watermarks.

Editing for YouTube, TikTok, and Instagram

YouTube Video Editing with Clipchamp

YouTube is the leading platform for long-form video content. To create compelling YouTube videos using Clipchamp:

1. **Choose the Right Aspect Ratio**: Select a 16:9 widescreen format to match YouTube's standard resolution.
2. **Import Media**: Drag and drop video clips, images, and audio files into Clipchamp.
3. **Trim & Arrange Clips**: Cut unnecessary parts and arrange sequences to create a smooth flow.
4. **Add Transitions & Effects**: Use fade-ins, cuts, and motion effects to maintain visual interest.
5. **Enhance with Text & Captions**: Add subtitles and on-screen text to make your video accessible and engaging.
6. **Apply Audio Adjustments**: Incorporate background music, adjust voiceover volume, and remove noise.
7. **Export in High Quality**: Export videos in 1080p for the best balance between quality and file size.

Pro Tip: Keep intros under 5 seconds to hook viewers quickly, and always include a strong call-to-action (CTA) at the end.

TikTok Video Editing with Clipchamp

TikTok thrives on short, engaging videos. When editing TikTok videos with Clipchamp:

1. **Use a Vertical Format (9:16)**: This optimizes your video for mobile viewing.
2. **Trim for Conciseness**: Keep videos between 7-15 seconds for maximum engagement.
3. **Apply Filters & Effects**: Use trendy color filters, glitch effects, and slow-motion features.
4. **Incorporate Text & Stickers**: Highlight key messages with animated text and overlays.

5. **Sync Video with Music**: Use Clipchamp's audio library or upload viral sounds to match the trends.
6. **Use Jump Cuts**: Maintain a fast pace to keep viewers engaged.
7. **Export and Upload in HD**: Ensure crisp visuals by exporting in high resolution.

Pro Tip: TikTok favors authentic, raw content, so avoid over-editing. Keep it simple and engaging.

Instagram Video Editing with Clipchamp

Instagram supports multiple video formats, including Stories, Reels, and IGTV. Here's how to optimize each type:

1. **Reels & Stories (9:16 format)**
   o Keep videos under 60 seconds.
   o Use built-in animations and effects to make them stand out.
   o Add text overlays to highlight key messages.
2. **Feed Videos (1:1 or 4:5 format)**
   o Ensure content is centered to avoid cropping.
   o Use professional-looking filters and branding elements.
   o Include captions to increase engagement.
3. **IGTV (16:9 or 9:16 format)**
   o For long-form content, maintain high quality (1080p resolution).
   o Ensure clear audio for an engaging viewing experience.

Pro Tip: Instagram's algorithm favors videos with early engagement, so add captions and ask viewers to interact in the first few seconds.

Best Practices for Engaging Social Media Content

1. Keep It Short and Engaging

Attention spans are short, so deliver key messages quickly. Start with a compelling hook within the first three seconds.

2. Use Captions and Subtitles

A significant portion of users watch videos without sound. Adding subtitles ensures accessibility and engagement.

3. Leverage Trends

Use trending music, hashtags, and effects to increase visibility on platforms like TikTok and Instagram.

4. Maintain Consistent Branding

Use brand colors, fonts, and styles consistently across all videos to strengthen recognition.

5. Include a Strong Call-to-Action (CTA)

Encourage viewers to like, comment, share, or subscribe at the end of your video.

6. Optimize for Mobile Viewing

Since most social media users browse on mobile devices, use vertical formats and high-contrast visuals for clarity.

Branding Videos with Logos and Watermarks

Branding ensures your content remains recognizable and professional. Here's how to add logos and watermarks in Clipchamp:

Adding a Logo Overlay

1. **Import Your Logo**: Upload a transparent PNG version of your logo into Clipchamp.
2. **Drag It onto the Timeline**: Place it in a corner where it won't obstruct important visuals.
3. **Adjust Opacity & Size**: Make the logo semi-transparent if needed for a subtle effect.
4. **Set Duration**: Extend it to appear throughout the video or only at key moments.

Creating a Watermark

1. **Use a Transparent Image**: Create a light, semi-transparent version of your logo.
2. **Overlay on the Entire Video**: Position it in a non-intrusive corner.
3. **Adjust Opacity**: Reduce transparency to avoid overpowering the main content.

Applying Branded Intros & Outros

1. **Design a Branded Intro**: Use Clipchamp's templates to add animated intros featuring your logo.
2. **End with a Call-to-Action**: Include an outro with social media links and a CTA to encourage engagement.

Pro Tip: Keep branding elements subtle yet consistent to avoid distracting viewers while reinforcing brand identity.

Conclusion

Clipchamp is a powerful tool for content creators and marketers looking to enhance their video editing workflow. By mastering platform-specific editing techniques, implementing best practices for engagement, and incorporating branding elements like logos and watermarks, you can create high-quality, professional videos that captivate audiences and strengthen brand presence.

Chapter 9: AI-Powered Features & Automations in Clipchamp

Introduction

In today's fast-paced digital world, AI-driven automation has revolutionized video editing, making it faster, more accessible, and more efficient. Clipchamp integrates powerful AI-powered features that enhance video production, streamline workflows, and elevate content quality with minimal effort. This chapter explores key AI-driven tools available in Clipchamp, how to use them effectively, and best practices for optimizing their impact on your videos.

1. AI Voiceovers: Transform Text into Professional Narration

What Are AI Voiceovers?

AI voiceovers allow you to convert text into lifelike speech, providing professional narration for your videos without requiring a microphone or recording experience. Clipchamp offers a variety of AI-generated voices in multiple languages and tones, making it an essential tool for content creators, marketers, and educators.

How to Use AI Voiceovers in Clipchamp

1. **Open Clipchamp** and start a new project.
2. Click on **Record & Create** and select **Text to Speech**.
3. Type or paste your script into the text box.
4. Choose the language, voice style, and speech speed.
5. Click **Preview** to listen and adjust settings if needed.
6. Click **Save to Media** and drag the AI-generated voiceover onto your timeline.

Best Practices for AI Voiceovers

- Keep sentences concise for better clarity.
- Select a voice tone that matches your video's style.
- Adjust speed for natural-sounding speech.
- Use punctuation strategically for better pauses and intonation.

2. Automatic Captions & Subtitles: Enhance Accessibility and Engagement

Benefits of AI-Generated Captions

Adding captions improves video accessibility, boosts engagement, and enhances SEO by making your content searchable. Clipchamp's automatic captioning tool uses AI to generate accurate subtitles in real time, reducing manual effort.

How to Add Auto-Generated Captions

1. Import or create your video in Clipchamp.
2. Click on **Captions & Subtitles** in the toolbar.
3. Select **Auto-Captions** and choose your language.
4. Click **Generate** and wait for the AI to transcribe your video.
5. Review and edit the captions for accuracy.
6. Customize font, size, and color to match your branding.

Best Practices for AI Captions

- Always proofread and correct any AI transcription errors.
- Use high-contrast colors for readability.
- Position captions where they don't obstruct key visuals.
- Optimize captions with keywords for better SEO ranking.

3. Smart Background Removal & Enhancement

What is AI Background Removal?

The AI-powered background removal feature allows users to replace or blur backgrounds effortlessly, eliminating the need for a green screen. This tool is ideal for professional presentations, gaming content, and social media videos.

How to Use AI Background Removal

1. Upload your video to Clipchamp.
2. Select the clip and click **Effects** in the toolbar.
3. Choose **Background Removal** and let the AI process the video.
4. Replace the background with an image, solid color, or video.
5. Adjust edge smoothing for a natural look.

Best Practices for Background Removal

- Use well-lit footage for better AI accuracy.
- Avoid busy backgrounds for cleaner results.
- Experiment with different replacement backgrounds to enhance storytelling.

Conclusion

AI-powered features in Clipchamp save time, enhance content quality, and improve accessibility. By leveraging **AI voiceovers**, **automatic captions**, and **background removal**, you can create high-quality videos effortlessly. Implement these AI tools in your workflow to produce professional, engaging, and SEO-optimized content efficiently.

Chapter 10: Troubleshooting & Performance Optimization

Exporting and rendering issues can be frustrating, especially when working with high-resolution videos or large projects. In this chapter, we'll cover how to **fix common Clipchamp export and rendering issues**, **boost performance on different devices**, and **manage large files effectively**.

1. Fixing Common Export and Rendering Issues

Video Export Stuck or Not Finishing

If your export process freezes or takes an unusually long time, try these solutions:
- **Restart Clipchamp & Your Device** – A simple restart clears system memory and resolves temporary glitches.
- **Check Storage Space** – Ensure you have **at least 10GB of free disk space** for smooth exporting.
- **Reduce Export Resolution** – If working with **4K or high-bitrate files**, try exporting in **1080p** or lower.
- **Use a Wired Internet Connection** – If you're exporting to the cloud, a **stable internet connection** is crucial.
- **Close Unused Applications** – Running too many programs can slow down rendering.

Video Preview is Lagging or Freezing

The preview window in Clipchamp may lag due to high processing demand. Fix it with these steps:
- **Lower the Playback Quality** – Change preview settings to "**Low Quality**" to improve performance.
- **Enable Hardware Acceleration** – Go to **Settings > Performance > Enable GPU acceleration**.
- **Use Proxy Files** – Work with lower-resolution versions of your clips to speed up editing.

Video Exports with No Sound

If your exported video is missing audio:
- **Check the Original File** – Ensure the **source audio is not muted or corrupted**.
- **Verify Audio Tracks in Timeline** – Ensure the correct **audio channel is selected** and not disabled.
- **Export in a Different Format** – Try exporting in **MP4 (AAC audio)** to resolve compatibility issues.

Blurry or Pixelated Video After Export

If your final video looks blurry, try these solutions:
- **Export at a Higher Bitrate** – Increase bitrate to **at least 8-12 Mbps for 1080p** videos.
- **Check Resolution Settings** – Ensure you are exporting at the correct resolution (**1920x1080 for HD, 3840x2160 for 4K**).
- **Use the Right Codec** – **H.264 MP4** provides the best balance of quality and compatibility.

2. Boosting Clipchamp Performance on Different Devices

Best Settings for Windows & Mac

To improve Clipchamp's performance on **Windows** or **Mac**, follow these steps:
- **Enable GPU Acceleration** – Use your **graphics card (GPU)** instead of the CPU for faster rendering.
- **Upgrade RAM** – At least **8GB RAM (16GB recommended for 4K editing)**.
- **Use an SSD** – Store your project files on an **SSD instead of an HDD** for faster read/write speeds.
- **Update Graphics Drivers** – Keep your **NVIDIA, AMD, or Intel GPU drivers** updated.

Best Performance on Mobile & Tablets

If using **Clipchamp on mobile** (Android/iOS):
- **Close Background Apps** – Free up system resources.
- **Lower Project Resolution** – **Edit in 720p or 1080p** instead of 4K to improve speed.
- **Keep Storage Free** – Ensure at least **5GB of free space** for smooth editing.

Best Performance on Chromebooks

Since **Chromebooks** rely on **web-based processing**, follow these tips:
- **Enable Hardware Acceleration** – Go to **Chrome Flags** and enable GPU acceleration.
- **Use a High-Speed Internet Connection** – Cloud rendering requires stable internet.

- **Close Other Browser Tabs** – Free up memory by reducing background tasks.

3. Managing Large Files Effectively

Compressing Video Files Without Losing Quality

- **Use Clipchamp's Compression Tool** – Lower file size while maintaining resolution.
- **Export in H.265 (HEVC) – 50% smaller file size** than H.264 with the same quality.
- **Reduce Bitrate Instead of Resolution** – Lower the bitrate slightly to reduce file size without affecting resolution.

Organizing Large Video Projects

- **Use an External Hard Drive** – Store large **source files** on an external SSD.
- **Delete Unused Clips** – Remove unnecessary footage to free up space.
- **Save Projects in the Cloud** – Use **Google Drive or OneDrive** to store backups.

Rendering Large Files Faster

- **Break Long Videos into Smaller Segments** – Edit in sections and merge them later.
- **Render Using Proxy Files** – Work with lower-resolution versions, then export in full quality.

- **Keep Your Computer Cool** – Overheating slows down performance; use a cooling pad if necessary.

4. Conclusion

By applying these **troubleshooting** and **optimization tips**, you can significantly improve Clipchamp's performance, fix common rendering issues, and manage large projects more efficiently. Whether you're exporting for **YouTube, social media, or professional use**, following the right steps ensures a **smooth editing workflow and high-quality output**.

11. Bonus Tips & Hidden Features

Clipchamp is packed with hidden gems that can boost your efficiency and creativity. In this chapter, we'll explore some **Easter eggs, shortcuts, and hidden features** that can help you get the most out of Clipchamp.

1. Easter Eggs and Lesser-Known Shortcuts

Hidden Shortcuts for Faster Editing

Mastering keyboard shortcuts can significantly speed up your workflow. Here are some lesser-known ones:

- **C** – Split clip at the playhead position (quick cut).
- **Shift + Up/Down Arrow** – Increase or decrease the clip's volume by 10%.
- **Alt + Scroll Wheel** – Zoom in and out on the timeline for better precision.
- **Shift + Drag** – Moves multiple clips at once, keeping them aligned.
- **Ctrl/Cmd + Shift + R** – Reverse the selected clip instantly.

Hidden UI Features

- **Right-Click Secrets** – Right-clicking clips in the timeline reveals extra options like "Replace Media," "Extract Audio," and "Duplicate."
- **Quick Text Animations** – When adding text, double-click on the text box and press "T" to instantly add animation.
- **Drag-and-Drop Effects** – You can drag video effects directly onto multiple clips at once instead of applying them one by one.

2. Enhancing Creativity with Stock Media & Effects

Using Clipchamp's Free Stock Library More Effectively

- **Search Filters** – When searching for stock videos, filter by **aspect ratio** and **resolution** to get clips that fit your project better.
- **Mix and Match Stock Elements** – Combine stock footage with overlays and text effects to create professional-looking intros.
- **Sound Effects & Music Syncing** – Use Clipchamp's **beat detection feature** to align music with scene transitions automatically.

Pro Editing Tricks with Effects

- **Glitch Effect Hack** – Add a flashing color filter and combine it with the "Shake" transition to create a **realistic glitch effect**.

- **Speed Ramping in a Manual Way** – Clipchamp doesn't yet have a built-in speed ramp tool, but you can fake it by **splitting a clip into sections and adjusting speed manually.**
- **Transparent Text Effect** – Layer a video over text and use the "Blend Mode" settings to create a **see-through text overlay.**

3. Community Resources and Further Learning

Clipchamp's Official Learning Hub

Clipchamp provides free tutorials and blog posts with updates on new features:

- **Blog:** Clipchamp Blog
- **YouTube Tutorials:** Clipchamp YouTube Channel

Online Communities for More Tips & Inspiration

- **Reddit:** Check out r/videoediting and r/Clipchamp for user discussions.
- **Facebook Groups:** Some communities share Clipchamp-specific editing tricks and templates.
- **Discord Servers:** Join general video editing Discord servers for real-time advice.

Expanding Your Editing Skills Beyond Clipchamp

- If you want to expand your editing skills further, learning software like **DaVinci Resolve, Premiere Pro, or CapCut** can help you level up.
- Understanding **color grading, storytelling techniques, and motion graphics** will improve the quality of your projects, even within Clipchamp's limits.